Stoicism

A Guide to Stoic Wisdom and Philosophy

Mark Roberts

Table of Contents

Introduction 1

Chapter 1: A Short Definition of Stoicism 5

Chapter 2: A Short History 6

Chapter 3: Key Aspects 14

Chapter 4: Applying Stoicism 27

Chapter 5: Famous Stoics 43

Chapter 6: On Stoicism, Law of Attraction, and Psychology.... 49

Chapter 7: Reflections and Meditations 55

Chapter 8: A Week with the Stoics 70

Chapter 9: Glossary of Terms 79

Conclusion 82

Introduction

"The chief task in life is simply this: To identify and separate matters so that I can say clearly to myself which are externals not under my control, and which have to do with the choices I actually control. Where then do I look for good and evil? Not to uncontrollable externals, but within myself to the choices that are my own."

- Epictetus

The Stoics were an emotionless bunch—or were they? The picture many people have when they think about this philosophy is of people enduring hardships with expressionless faces and endless, emotionless patience. Even happy occasions would not cause exuberance to a Stoic if you believe the popular picture painted of them.

That is, however, not the whole truth about the philosophy of Stoicism. While patience certainly is a virtuosic principle, it was only one of a whole list of virtues necessary to be a good human being according to the philosophy. To *be* and *do* good is the whole objective of living.

They also certainly did not avoid emotion but, believed in controlling it. To the Stoics, emotions are the only things that lie within human control and as such, should be guarded and shaped to be useful as tools on the road to becoming a virtuous person.

Stoicism is being rediscovered in modern society, and a resurgence of this philosophy can be found on countless websites, blogs, and online groups. There is something to say regarding the moral and ethical questions we are confronted with today, for anyone prepared to listen.

A Google search on modern Stoicism delivers almost two million results. Some people speculate that the reason for the new popularity lies in the fact that Stoicism is concerned with reality, not fantasy or idealism. It wants to teach believers how to embrace challenges and make a success, rather than retreating into physical or mental refuges.

In an era where an increasing number of people live into old age, health issues are real concerns. Chronic pain afflicts ever younger people, with diseases such as arthritis, cancer, and diabetes on the rise. Stoicism tackles the problems of pain and physical discomfort head-on.

Academics and psychotherapists founded a movement called Modern Stoicism in 2012, in the United Kingdom. They offer events such as annual conferences, training, and a blog about applying Stoic principles to modern life.

An international group called the Stoic Fellowship calculates that seven continents now have followers of the Stoic lifestyle.

Every October, they pull people from all over the world together for what they call a Stoic Week. During this time, people discuss their practical experiences with the philosophy. The information gathered during the week is used in research to put together their training courses on mindfulness and Stoic resilience.

In the digital age, the dissemination of information is easier than ever before, and Stoicism is benefiting from it. In addition to the availability of information, many social structures have changed or collapsed totally. Societies have new lifestyles and thought patterns. Institutions such as churches, which were emotional and cognitive anchors in the lives of individuals, became eroded and have even disappeared in some instances. Many family units can't fulfill their roles anymore and the prevalence of divorce shatters the stability older generations took for granted.

Modern people often complain they feel lost and without a moral compass to guide them. Stoicism has stepped in to provide much-needed grounding and ethical guidance.

Some aspects of Stoicism fit in seamlessly with the resurgence of self-help movements and the renewed interest in spiritualism.

The philosophy turns the eye inward to focus on conditions and responses that can be controlled, instead of fixating on external events that are not within the sphere of human control.

It is more accessible than some of the Eastern belief systems because no special training or isolated retreats are needed to practice Stoicism. It does not cost a lot of money to acquire basic knowledge and can be applied immediately.

Aspects of Stoicism can be seen in cognitive behavioral therapy, which is a practical application of psychotherapy that many people find useful. It neutralizes the victim mentality that some people follow as the road of least resistance, and advocates taking responsibility for your own life and decisions. A difficult childhood, poor circumstances, and political discrimination are all swept aside in favor of standing up morally and making the right choices.

There is much to be said for the Stoic way of thinking in our rushed digital age. Keep reading and enjoy discovering the relevance of ancient wisdom.

Chapter 1: A Short Definition of Stoicism

Stoicism is a school of philosophical thought with a clear framework of ethical principles.

The means through which the Stoics arrive at their ethical beliefs are logic and reasoning.

They derive their logic from Nature and the natural world.

Happiness is to be found in a virtuous life, through doing good to others and the community at large, and staying in the present moment.

Stoicism views all humans as equals and the Cosmos as part of one divine being that dictates the natural laws according to which humans should live.

Moderation in all things is a key point.

Stoicism flourished until about 3 CE, after which Christianity, which was adopted as the state religion, caused its decline. It saw a revival in the Renaissance, and again is experiencing a resurgence in our modern society.

Chapter 2: A Short History

Stoicism originated in Greece around 300 BCE. It was founded by Zeno of Citium (335–263 BCE). During his lifetime, his philosophy had a great influence on Hellenistic and Roman ethical thinking.

The principles of Stoicism tried to make sense out of everyday occurrences and provide guidelines for the best way to live one's life. They were very much concerned with ethics, science, and the effective application of logic.

The Early Days

Zeno was born in Citium, which is now known in modern times as Cyprus. After finishing his schooling, he became a merchant. Among other things, he traded in the rare—and very expensive—purple dye the Greeks obtained from sea snails. He became very wealthy in this trade because the dye was seen as a symbol of luxury. It was sought after by the likes of the wealthy and royal.

On a trading voyage in about 312 BCE, he was shipwrecked and stranded in Athens. According to the centuries-old stories, Zeno traveled to the Oracle of Delphi to ask for advice. There, he was told to dye himself not with the colors of the sea, but with the colors of dead men. He interpreted this as a sign that he should submerge himself in the teachings of the ancient wise men and philosophers.

He became well-versed in the works of some of the foremost philosophers, especially Socrates (470–399 BCE). He ended up studying with the Cynic philosopher Crates of Thebes (365–285 BCE) for some decades, learning the values of living virtuously and in harmony with Nature.

He also attended the world-famous Academy, which was the world's first university. The Platonic Academy, or simply The Academy, was founded by the philosopher Plato (c. 428–c. 347 BCE) in 387 BCE. Plato inherited the land just outside of Athens and started holding regular discussions with friends and colleagues about philosophy and matters of the day. Over time, it evolved into a more structured gathering. The Academy stood until its destruction in 86 BCE.

Eventually, Zeno felt ready to start his own school of philosophy, and he chose as his classroom a famous landmark in Athens called the Painted Colonnade, or Painted Porch. In Greek, the Painted Porch is called the *Stoa Poikilê*, and this is echoed in the name of Zeno's system of thinking, Stoicism.

The Painted Porch stretched along the north side of the Athenian Agora, or, old marketplace. The porch was fronted by Doric columns on the outside and Ionic columns on the inside. The walls were lined with panels of paintings by the most famous classical Greek artists, depicting Athenian war triumphs.

Zeno taught his followers that the universe was governed by divine reason, and the only way to be happy was to conform to that reasoning.

Unfortunately, not many of the early writings of the movement survived; but we do know that Zeno was succeeded by Cleanthes (c. 330–c. 230 BCE) as head of the school after the latter's death, who was then followed by Chrysippus (279–206 BCE). These three are considered the original Stoics.

Life in Greece changed irrevocably after the deaths of Aristotle (384–322 BCE) and Alexander the Great (356–323 BCE). Athens ceased to be the center of the civilized world and other cities such as Rome, Pergamum, and Alexandria became more prominent.

The earlier politics of virtue, order, and a close relationship between cosmic and civic values were replaced by uncertainty and moral values that held little conviction.

In this stormy sea of changing circumstances and thought patterns, the Stoics tried to restore balance. They put the emphasis again on living simply and close to nature through the application of reason to find happiness, while moving away from using logic as an empty end in itself.

Socrates, Plato, and Aristotle

Although very little of the early Stoic writings survived, we know that the famed philosophers Socrates, Plato, and Aristotle influenced the development of Stoicism. The Stoic concept of wisdom was the third big classical system to be developed.

Little is known about Socrates' life in Athens, and the information we have comes from other philosophers' texts. His biggest academic contribution was what has become known as the Socratic method, teaching his students by way of question-and-answer. As the discussion progressed, so did the student's understanding of the concept develop and deepen. The method is rooted in Socrates' belief that all answers are attainable through reason and logical deduction. Students gradually discovered the contradictions in their arguments and worked toward solid conclusions.

Plato was a student of Socrates. His theory of forms, with which he tried to reconcile the changing nature of the world with its permanent nature, can be seen in the Stoic concepts of natural law and physics. The theory of forms posits that there is a difference between the changing world we experience with our senses and the 'real' world behind it that does not change. The unchanging world 'seen' with the mind consists of forms that point the way to what we perceive every day.

Aristotle studied at Plato's Academy in Athens from the age of eighteen. His theory of universals influenced many philosophers, including Zeno. He focused on the properties of things; qualities inherent to their being. He used the word 'universal' to denote the characteristics specific things have in common. For Aristotle, there was no division between universals and things, as there was for Plato. According to Aristotle, properties can only exist if they are bound to something. He used logic to identify universals and describe every aspect of things and their properties. This system of logical reasoning was employed and refined by the Stoics.

Developments After Zeno

During the period between the second and early first centuries BCE, Middle Stoicism reigned. The founders of the Middle Stoa, the philosopher, Panaetius (c. 180–109 BCE), and his disciple, Posidonius (c.135–51 BCE), linked Stoic doctrines to moral issues like duty and obligation, as well as the study of nature. This appealed to Romans in the first two centuries CE, who had a very practical outlook on life, and so the philosophy became very popular in Rome. More specifically, some of the most prominent Roman figures were known to be followers of this school of thought.

The best-known Roman Stoic philosophers included teachers such as Epictetus (55–c. 135 CE), or politicians, such as the statesman, Lucius Seneca (4 BCE–65 CE), and Roman emperor, Marcus Aurelius (121–180 CE). The base focus of the movement became more practical, rather than theoretical. Concepts such as their outlook on marriage and family life evolved during this time to become more positive.

It is believed that the Stoic scholars tried during this period to reconcile their movement to the ideas they thought were correct in other philosophies.

The emphasis on the practical application of the philosophy remained in the later stage of the movement. Through the writings of people such as Marcus Aurelius—most associated today with his pivotal work, *Meditations*—it became clear that Stoic teachings were just as popular as Christianity. Their philosophy was much more than mere thinking; it was a way of *being*. They believed that getting to know the true value of nature and the universe led to transformation, which was in a way similar to the Christian teachings of the time.

Stoicism remained popular well into the Middle Ages. The philosopher Boethius (d. 324/325 CE), wrote about the essence of good and evil, freedom, and chance. He tried to reconcile humans' free will with divine foreknowledge, and his writings glorified reason as a means to escape the difficulties of life.

Other thinkers of the Middle Ages, such as Lactantius (240–320 CE), wrestled with God's righteous anger against transgressors and the rewards promised for the faithful, against the Stoic concept of remaining unperturbed by any emotions.

They advocated the equality of all people and the need to live by what they called the natural laws. That exerted great influence on the political systems of the time, as well as those to follow during the Renaissance.

The period from the late 1500s through the early 1700s is known as Neostoicism. The leading philosopher was Justus Lipsius (1547-1606), who tried to create a combination of Stoic doctrines and Christianity. It was a time in history that saw many upheavals and religious wars, and Lipsius tried to provide a framework to help ordinary people make sense of the hardships they were facing.

Stoicism declined when Christianity became the dominant doctrine, but aspects of their philosophy remained in Western culture, experiencing a revival in the late 20th century.

The modern applications of Stoic philosophy will be discussed in a later chapter.

The Influence on Christianity

It is no wonder that some concepts of Stoicism seem to be echoed in Christian doctrines. Stoicism actively thrived through the centuries in which Christian doctrines were being developed. Such concepts include the immaterial view of the soul, judgment, conscience, the importance of natural laws, the value of human life, and self-control.

There are even claims about a correspondence between the apostle Paul (c. 4 BCE–c. 64 CE) and Seneca, although the eight letters are now widely accepted as being forgeries due to many inconsistencies. It is, however, true that Paul was very well acquainted with Stoic teachings and some of them likely influenced his writings.

Chapter 3: Key Aspects

"The philosopher's lecture room is a hospital: You ought not to walk out of it in a state of pleasure, but in pain—for you are not in good condition when you arrive!"

- Epictetus

Stoic philosophy invented the canonical three parts of philosophy. These are ethics, physics, and logic. To the first Stoics, ethics were the only worthwhile reason to study philosophy, and ethical principles were supported by physics and logic. These areas are explored through practicing the primary virtues.

The virtues are practical wisdom (*sofia*), justice (*dikaiosune*), courage (*andreia*), and moderation (*sophrosyne*). Some Stoics believed the four to be interdependent with wisdom as the underlying and connecting element, while others put wisdom alone at the top with the other three as subdivisions.

In addition to the main virtues, there is also a list of secondary desirable traits:

- Under the primary virtue of practical wisdom: Good judgment, the ability to make a good practical assessment, a quick moral sense, discretion, shrewdness, and resourcefulness

- Under the primary virtue of moderation: A good sense of the order in which things should be done, propriety, a sense of honor, and self-control

- Under the primary virtue of courage: Confidence, perseverance, mental toughness, magnanimity, and a sense of understanding what needs to be done, regardless of circumstances

- Under the primary virtue of justice: Sociability, kindness, piety, and good companionship

Stoics liked ordered lists that were easy to memorize, and so in addition to these two schemes, they also referred to a threefold set of rules to live life by. Epictetus listed them as the Discipline of Ascent, the Discipline of Action, and the Discipline of Desire and Aversion.

Stoics believe human beings are naturally inclined to develop morally correct behaviors. Through the application of reason, these behaviors are modified throughout an adult's life. They don't distinguish between the rational and emotional aspects but view them as integrated to form a balanced and whole personality.

Ethics

Central to the Stoic view on ethics are the concepts of self-control, duty, and unity. Their interpretation of these doctrines brought them in confrontation with the Epicureans, the Skeptics, and the Christians.

- The followers of the philosopher Epicurus (341–270 BCE) believed the best thing a human being can do is to pursue pleasure to bring freedom from pain and fear, and lead to emotional equilibrium and tranquility. They differ from Hedonism in that pleasure was not advocated to be without bounds. According to Epicurus, friendship, knowledge, and living virtuously should moderate pleasure. Moderation included staying away from politics and world affairs for Epicureans.

- The Skeptics, led by Pyrrho (c. 360–270 BCE), held the view that no virtue or sincerity can motivate human behavior. The only factor that could influence people's choices was self-interest, rejecting rational thought and reasoning as means to a good life.

- Christianity taught that nothing but God and his Son, Jesus, may take center stage in one's life. To them, wisdom could only be given by God, and no human being was capable of discerning the truth about the world or living a righteous life through their own mental efforts.

The Stoics identify the instincts for self-preservation and self-knowledge as the primary impulses which motivate human behavior. They believe these are imparted by nature and every newborn creature is equipped with them.

All creatures start from the same footing, according to the Stoics, but only humans develop rational thought and learn about concepts such as virtue and duty as they mature. This brings an awareness of other people such as the family, community, and eventually all of mankind.

This awareness shapes a human's interaction with nature and the aim should be to fulfill the required roles in these groups in harmony with the laws of nature. That will lead to what is known as human flourishing (*eudaimonia*).

Stoic doctrines do not attach emotional value to any concepts except virtue and vice. Anything other than these is described as 'indifferents' by Stoic writers. The presence of any indifferents is immaterial to reaching the state of *eudaimonia*, but some indifferents are more desirable than others. Every indifferent which crosses a person's life path is a stepping-stone to make the next choice on the path to either the harmonic life or the opposite thereof.

Suffering and unhappiness can be attributed to bad choices, also known as passions. These are decisions made with bad judgments that create conflict with the natural way things were designed. Such decisions cause distress and anxiety, and the conflict can only be resolved by employing reason to change the person's course of life.

Regarding the ethics of the concept, it is important to note that Stoics believe humans have no power to influence the unfolding of history by their actions. They teach the pre-ordination of the universe by a divine force. The only choice humans have and should make, is to choose their responses to events. The choices made determine the course our lives take.

Physics

The second leg on which the attainment of *eudaimonia* rests is physics. It comes from the Greek word *fusis* and does not mean the same as the modern interpretation of the word.

To a Stoic, physics is the belief that everything that has ever existed, and everything that will ever exist, does so as One in a Divine Fire. This One, the Cosmos and everything in it, possesses a dualistic nature of being active and passive at once. Everything that exists can act *and* be acted upon. Nothing without a body exists in this world.

The active force of the Cosmos is called reason (*logos*) and is described as a fire that generates the four basic elements the universe consists of—fire, air, earth, and water. Fire and air are seen as active components that form the breath of life (*pneuma*), while earth and water are more passive. These elements interact with one another and occupy the same space at the same time, one and the same, yet never fully becoming one another.

The concept of *pneuma* is central in the Stoic theory about physics and is the primary binding force of all existing matter. All objects and concepts in the universe are classified according to the degree and the type of *pneuma* activity they have.

At the basic level is cohesion (*hexis*), which denotes the state of being found in inanimate objects that are merely held together by their *pneuma*, without any activity. Things that grow and reproduce without any cognitive abilities such as plants have *hexis* as well as growth (*fusis*), together with their *pneuma*. Animals that have cognitive activity, as well as instincts, possess both *hexis* and *fusis*, as well as soul (*psyche*).

Humans are at the top of the chain because they have *logos* and *psyche*. We have the ability to reason and are in possession of a soul. It was believed that the soul survives physical death, but eventually perishes in the world conflagration.

Qualities like justice and virtue are considered gifts from *pneuma*.

Concerning the Cosmos, early Stoics believed everything went through an eternal cyclic pattern of creation, flourishing, decline, and a final conflagration.

Logic

The concept of logic was straightforward in early Stoic thinking. Everything started with a basic statement that was either truthful or false. Through the knowledge acquired about harmonious living and applying reason, the statement had to be examined and accepted or rejected.

Stoic logic can be divided into two parts, sayables and assertables.

- Sayables are statements that can be true or false and have no specific structure in themselves.

- Assertibles are statements that are complete in themselves because they have structure and are true.

In Stoicism, the ability to use logic effectively marks the difference between being wise and being foolish. It enables the listener to discern when statements are mere speculation or to make ambiguous statements clearer.

A historian called Diogenes Laertius (c. 200–250 CE) divided Stoic logic into four parts:

Earnestness

The logical way is to keep an open mind about anything until you know the truth for sure because you might be wrong in your assumptions. The truth will be established once a statement is measured against the right reason.

Knowledge

Knowledge is having a position that no argument can shake. If you have any valid points of view that have to be shifted or negated if the new statement is accepted, the new statement might not be the truth.

Wariness

Wariness asks you to examine any presumptions held about the proposed statement. Are there any general considerations that should be taken into account when weighing the truth of it?

Appropriate Assent

Appropriate assent is considering any surrounding truths before declaring a new statement as true. Are there other proven facts that have to be taken into account?

The Four Primary Virtues

The origins of the four cardinal virtues of wisdom, justice, courage, and moderation can be traced as far back as Socrates. Visually they were represented in a tetramorph of four animals. A man symbolized wisdom, an eagle symbolized justice, courage was symbolized by a lion, and moderation's symbol was a bull.

Diogenes described the four virtues as the only elements needed for an honorable life. He reasoned that a life lived with wisdom, justice, courage, and moderation will enable the person to live up to their full potential. That alone, Diogenes said, is worthy of being called good.

At the heart of the Stoic concept of wisdom lies their desire to be able to distinguish between events they can control and events that are beyond their control. The famous Roman writer and scholar, Cicero (106–43 BCE), said that a man who has virtue will not need anything else. A virtuous life will fulfill every desire a man can have, be it fame, fortune, or finding the meaning of life because it brings wisdom.

Being wise enough to know what to do still requires courage to do it. To the ancient Stoics, it sometimes literally meant facing death. The Roman senator, Publius Clodius Thrasea Paetus, for instance, was killed in 66 CE for his opposition to the tyrannical rule of the emperor Nero (37–68 CE).

Justice is the underlying motivation for being wise and courageous. The Roman emperor Marcus Aurelius, who reigned from 161 to 180 CE, regarded justice as the source of the other three virtues.

Cicero said the same with his well-known expression *summum bonum* (for the highest good). To the Stoics, justice was to be understood in a much wider sense than we use the word today. To them, it meant to act honorably toward fellow men and do no harm.

The basis for justice is their concept of *sympatheia*, which means the oneness of all that exists. Aurelius said anything that injures the hive, injures the bee too. Epictetus is quoted as saying, "Seeking the very best in ourselves means actively caring for the welfare of other human beings."

This immediately leads to the virtue of moderation or self-control. Aristotle called this the "golden mean," lying between excess and lack. The Stoics believe having just enough to fulfill the essentials is the secret to contentment.

Moderation and self-control also extend to emotions and experiences, cautioning against any extremes or relying on swiftly disappearing sources of pain or pleasure.

The Three Disciplines

Keeping the main goal of Stoicism in mind, which is living in balance and harmony with nature, the three disciplines look at doing exactly that from different perspectives.

The Discipline of Assent

Assent (*synkatathesis*) is about living a virtuous life according to one's inner voice of reason and freedom. It comprises truthful words and actions that are derived from the awareness of one's true nature.

This awareness will allow you to stand back from any passions or vices before assenting or agreeing to them.

This discipline is also sometimes known as Stoic Mindfulness, but it should not be confused with the Buddhist practice of mindfulness. In Stoic terms, it means paying attention (*prosochê*) to the mind's faculty of reasoning to achieve a harmonious life.

The Discipline of Desire

This is also called Stoic Acceptance and is probably the closest to what is generally called a stoic view of life.

It means resisting any unhealthy and irrational desire (*orexis*) that would have made a life in harmony with nature, following the principles of physics, impossible.

This can be misleading though because it could paint a picture of Stoics as having no backbone. That is far from the truth and there are examples throughout history of Stoics having accepted their fate with a great deal of courage and determination.

The Discipline of Action

This can be seen as the virtue of living with other human beings in such a way that all achieve *eudaimonia*. The Greek word used for action, *hormê*, actually means the impulse that starts an action.

If the discipline of action is seen as an extension of Stoic ethics, then wishing every human being a flourishing life is the impulse that drives virtuous actions.

They also accepted that the ultimate result of their wishes is not within their control, so they added the reserve "God willing." In doing so, the Stoics combined their exhortation to rigorous and courageous action with a philosophical acceptance of the Divine Fire that created the Cosmos.

Marcus Aurelius wrote that Stoics should always remember this reserve, and act for the welfare of all humankind, to add value. This discipline is also called the Stoic Philanthropy.

Chapter 4: Applying Stoicism

"Between stimulus and response, there is a space. In that space is our power to choose our response."

- Viktor Frankl

Although Stoicism was developed in a world that looked completely different from our current reality, it encompasses timeless principles that hold true in any society.

The ancient philosophy has seen a big revival in recent years, with many well-known politicians, authors, actors, and business people expressing the importance Stoicism has in their lives.

Stoic principles team up well with modern psychology and as such, have found many practical uses.

Identify the Things You Can Control

A cornerstone of Stoic philosophy is the notion that it is essential to distinguish between events within our control and those that are not.

We cannot direct and change events that happen outside ourselves. Stoicism teaches that only emotions, and the underlying intentions to action, are totally within our sphere of control.

That should not be confused with passiveness or submissiveness. Take the example of a business trip that goes awry because the plane gets delayed. In the planning stages of the trip, a business executive was not passive at all. Careful plans were made, itineraries were drawn up, and schedules upon arrival were finalized.

The executive arrives at the airport on time only to find that the plane will be two hours late due to a big and unexpected thunderstorm. All the diligently laid plans come to nothing and hasty adjustments have to be made.

No amount of shouting at the airport staff, or phoning the management of the airline, will change the situation. The only things the executive has control over, are their responses to the challenge. Emotions, words, and personal actions such as calmly making new plans, are the only things the executive can control.

A Practical Exercise

The power of journaling really comes into its own when trying to work the dichotomy inherent in control out. Journaling can be helpful to any person of any age who wants to properly take stock of his day, and reflect on how to do it differently tomorrow.

Epictetus told his students to write philosophy down every day because writing is the heart of philosophy. It was seen as a practical exercise in grounding themselves in Stoic teachings.

Seneca told a friend that he liked to journal at night after the house had gone quiet, and everyone else had gone to sleep. After examining his whole day in brutal honesty, he went to bed and enjoyed refreshing and peaceful sleep.

The Greeks had a tradition of making notes for themselves about anything they read or heard. They did this to capture phrases or concepts that were important to them, to reflect upon them later, and memorize them.

Journaling for reflection, rather than memorizing, was a logical step for the Stoics to take. They refined the art of personal writing to mirror their day that had passed and provide a space for mental preparation for the day to come.

It is recommended to reread journal entries periodically. Comprehension of the Stoic way of thinking and living does not always happen in a sudden epiphany. For most people, experiences and small insights build on each other like blocks. Revisiting previous journal entries highlights the blocks so that eventually, a strong and beautiful clarity can arise.

In preparing for your day that lies ahead, it can be helpful to utilize a form of envisioning, as well as meditation. In a later chapter, you will find some example meditations to get you started.

Envisioning can be part of your writing. It boils down to writing your day's story, as you would like it to unfold. You can also watch the scenes play out in your mind like a movie. Experience the feelings that would go with the events you envision. Smell the smells and hear the sounds. Make the picture real in your mind.

Before you end that day, replay your mind movie and see how much of what you envisioned that morning came true. Reflect on where and how you could have responded to something in a different way, more in accordance with Stoic principles. Maybe you tried to change an event that was out of your control.

Go ahead and practice journaling a few days a week. Remember, Stoicism is a philosophy of actions, not only thoughts.

You Create Your Own Emotions

In one of the passages from Marcus Aurelius' *Meditations*, he talks about how it is impossible to escape anxiety. Rather, he said, we should say we discarded anxiety because it is inside us and not an external force.

Emotions are our responses to events happening to and around us. They are formed out of our perceptions of what the real world is.

Something that arises within us can be changed by us. Change your perception and your world changes. Things you believe in acquire power over you from that belief. Following Stoic principles means to remind yourself constantly about the power you have over your emotions. This peaceful, powerful, and undisturbed state of mind was called *apatheia* in ancient times.

Emotions are one of the only things we can control, and one of the only things we should worry about controlling. External events are beyond our management and should not cause us sleepless nights.

A Few Practical Steps to Mastery of the Emotions

Theodore Roosevelt (1858–1919) always reminded his troops about the importance of having steady nerves. While you might say that is easier said than done, the first American astronauts in the 1960s were trained not to panic.

NASA's modus operandi is actually quite simple. It involves having a *feeling* of control.

The would-be astronauts were repeatedly put through anything that the scientists imagined they might have to face in space.

They were faced with life and death scenarios multiple times during a day's training.

Eventually, they became so adept at handling any possible problems, that their heart rates and blood pressure steadied when faced with a potential crisis, instead of rising. That gave them clear heads and enabled better decision-making. It made them confident in their abilities to control their situation.

Samurais recognize, too, that the most important part of their training is not with a sword, but in learning to keep a level head. That leads to the next practical step, which is emotional preparation.

Suzuki Shosan (1579–1655), who was one of the greatest samurais in history, admonished students to beware of allowing the mind to give in to the mind; it is the mind itself that confuses the mind in the first place, according to Shosan.

They achieved calm through hard training, imagining the worst and getting it over with, and resuming training to meet the worst head-on. Ancient Stoicism called this technique negative visualization. The Latin term by which it is known is *premeditatio malorum.*

This technique is used to this day to train special forces the world over. They also utilize the third practical step, which is breathing.

We tend to think about breathing as something automatic, not worth considering because it just happens on its own. Learning to do what is known as meditation breathing, however, has been shown to bring clarity of mind, increase attention span, and boost happiness.

Meditation, or mindful, breathing is *focusing* on inhaling and exhaling, to the exclusion of anything else. Become conscious of the rhythm of your breathing and experience every breath fully. Make it an emotional anchor to come back to at any time it feels like emotions are going to overwhelm you.

Does learning to inhibit your emotions mean you must be without empathy for others? Not at all! Empathy is simply controlled emotions that lead to compassionate acts. All human beings are equal and should be treated equally well.

There Are Always Choices

Recognizing that you have control over some things—but not everything—brings with it mindfulness. You have to be present in the moment to evaluate whether the current situation and its associated events can be changed, or if you can only choose your response to it.

Getting frustrated about outside events that can't be changed breeds unhappiness and other negative emotions. Experiencing a constant barrage of negative emotions is not only damaging to mental health but can also harm physical health.

Choices in Practice

In practical terms, embracing Stoic philosophical principles will empower you to harness your inner power. It will bring about the opposite of a victim mentality where people get so overwhelmed by circumstances that they lapse into passivity.

The first question you have to ask yourself is whether the situation you have to decide about is really under your control. If the answer is yes, completely, you have to discern whether any of the four virtues are involved. Does the decision provide an opportunity to practice wisdom, courage, justice, or moderation?

If the situation does not involve any virtues, it is one of the indifferents. Remember that an indifferent is something that does not impact any aspect of morals or character, but rather serves as a stepping-stone on your path in which you may have to make a choice.

The last question to ask then would be whether it is an indifferent that is preferable to pursue without causing conflict with virtue, or whether it should be avoided. Avoidance is only an option if doing so will not result in a conflict with any of the virtues.

Should the answer to the first question about control be yes, but only partially, it is necessary to decide whether an attempt should be made and if such an attempt has a reasonable chance of success.

Overcoming Fear

We have seen that emotions are one of the only things we really have control over, and fear is an extremely strong emotion.

What does a Stoic do when fear has taken hold? Seneca wrote, "We are more often frightened than hurt; and we suffer more from imagination than from reality."

Even imaginary fears can, unfortunately, have consequences that have to be dealt with. Referring back to the section on creating your own emotions, your essential steps are visualization, planning, and preparing for the worst you can imagine happening regarding the situation you are afraid of.

Putting Your Plan into Action

It is always helpful to write down your thoughts. Your journal might be the go-to notebook for you. Whether you choose to write in a journal or not, the key concept to understand is that you have to be honest with yourself. Don't deny your feelings their legitimacy. Stoics don't avoid feelings, they master them.

Admit that the scale of your fear is out of control at that moment. Do not beat yourself up about that, but rather accept it as it is, and tell yourself it is temporary.

Next, start writing down possible solutions that would end the fear. Don't focus on any reasons why a solution won't work—brainstorm with yourself on any possibility without judging the merit.

The next practical step is to look at every possibility written down in the previous step, objectively. Try to work out what is needed to make it a workable plan. Write the steps for implementation down and if they tick all the boxes, put your plan in motion.

Center on Principles and Character

For a practicing Stoic, virtues and virtuous living are the most important things in their lives. Wealth, position, or fame will pass and be forgotten. Principles and character, on the other hand, will always be remembered.

Marcus Aurelius was fond of reminding himself that he could die anytime, so life has to be lived as if it will be the last day.

On one of the archaeological digs in ancient Rome, a statue of a tall man in a long toga was discovered. The man had a regal bearing and was obviously an emperor. There was only one problem: The statue had no head.

On closer examination, the scientists saw the statue had been designed to have a detachable head. The only explanation was that a new head was made every time a new emperor came to the throne. Roman emperors were very important and powerful, but not important enough to have a whole statue dedicated to them.

That is a sobering thought to anyone thinking their current station in life will be an enduring legacy.

A Practical Reflection

The ancient Stoics had a practice called *memento mori*. It means to remember the dead. It might sound like a somber and macabre pastime, but the origins go back to Socrates, who said the proper practice of philosophy is about death and dying.

Although that could seem harsh and grim, reflecting on dying from time to time will help to keep perspective on life events.

It promotes humility and renews an appetite for living. It also brings an element of urgency to our plans and a willingness to examine our motivations for those plans with honesty.

"Not My Circus, Not My Monkeys…"

This humorous expression has become the modern way of saying, "I don't have control over what you do, and I refuse to stress about it."

Stoicism teaches the same principle. Emotions and responses are every person's own responsibility, and trying to take on another's emotions, or to join them in complaining, does that person no favors.

Let's look for a moment at what is at the heart of complaining. It is essentially blame-shifting. It exempts the complainant from looking at his or her own response to the other person's behavior. If you believe your indignation is justified, you are the victim of someone else, and often passivity follows hot on the heels of feeling that way.

Instead, Stoic philosophy teaches that the other person's actions and feelings are not your problems. Only your response to them is your problem.

A certain degree of detachedness is necessary.

Putting This in Practice

The motivational speaker Will Bowen started a no-complaints challenge in 2006, and it has since grown to engage thousands of followers.

He asked a few people in his community to go for 21 days without uttering one single complaint. This caught on like wildfire and since then, more than 13 million people have taken the challenge.

Bowen says it takes the average person four to eight months to complete the 21 days without complaining. Complaining is a habit that is hard to break, but it is worth doing.

Marcus Aurelius wrote in his *Meditations* that Stoics should look inward, not outward. Complaining and meddling in the affairs of others shifts the mind's eye outward. Confucius is reported to have said of a man who complained bitterly about another's behavior, that the complainant surely must be a worthy man, but he who is Confucius has no time for complaining; he has too much soul-searching to do.

It all comes down to the fundamental distinction between what is in our control, and what is beyond it.

Epictetus' advice when tempted to complain is to simply take a step back first, and look at the big picture while holding a feeling of gratitude for everything that is going right.

Enjoy Life Now

Life isn't always exactly the way we want it to be, but there are many things that can be enjoyed if you are prepared to really see them.

Modern society tells us we can have it all and that, indeed, we should have it all. Many people have become trapped in a materialistic, consumer-centered way of living. Anything can be acquired, used up, and discarded for something new.

Stoic values, on the other hand, teach us that there are only a few things worth our attention and time. If we have those, life can be enjoyed with appreciation and gratitude.

It brings calmness because there is no need to chase after the next and best possession or experience.

On the Practical Side

The Stoic exercise of *amor fati*, or loving fate, was used by ancient teachers to show their students what contentment with the 'now' means.

The core concept to grasp here is to make the best out of anything that comes your way. Aurelius said a fire burns brightly with everything that is thrown in it.

It means being at peace with all circumstances, accepting that they are unfolding as they should.

Making a daily list of things to be grateful for, goes a long way in focusing the attention on how precious the present moment is.

Observe and Listen with Gratitude

Marcus Aurelius often admonished himself to keep an open mind, like a beginner in the study of human behavior. Observe the world and the people around you without any preconceived ideas.

You will learn far more with such an attentive attitude. Keep in mind the Stoic belief that everything in the universe is one. There is a relationship between fellow human beings and between humans and nature.

Never stop reading and apply what you read to events in your life, as well as to your thoughts.

Observe in the deep tranquil state of mind that only comes through gratitude.

The Practice of Gratitude

In keeping with Stoic teachings, we should cultivate a habit of being grateful for everything and everyone that comes into our lives—even the mishaps, annoyances, and unfortunate events.

Seeing your life with the full perspective of everything happening will show you the real interconnectedness of all that exists.

The impact of bad happenings sometimes brings far better things than we ever imagined.

- Observe the things to be grateful for every day and write them down in your journal

- Watch your language and use the words of a grateful and happy person when you speak, not the words of an unhappy and embittered individual

- Practice gratitude rituals, such as saying grace before a meal; you do not have to be religious to give thanks for the food you are about to eat, it merely brings awareness of how blessed life is

- Express your appreciation frequently to others, where it is needed

- Express concrete gratitude by doing things for others

- Notice the beauty in nature

- Try the 21-day challenge of no complaints

Chapter 5: Famous Stoics

In addition to the ancient philosophers who started and developed the Stoic doctrines, many other well-known historical figures from all walks of life were Stoics or were influenced by Stoic thinking.

Political and Military Figures

Several American presidents have been Stoics or have admitted to being inspired by Stoic principles.

George Washington, Thomas Jefferson, Theodore Roosevelt, and Franklin D. Roosevelt are on this list.

George Washington

One of America's founding fathers, Washington (1732–1799) was known for exceptional composure and self-discipline. He did not grow up wealthy and had no formal education, but he was exposed to Stoicism by his friends and later in-laws, the Fairfax family.

He took Cato as his role model, as depicted in a 1712 play by Joseph Addison called *Cato, a Tragedy*. Washington watched numerous performances of the play and often quoted lines from it.

Thomas Jefferson

Although there is some doubt in literary circles whether Jefferson (1743–1826) really was a Stoic, or if he rather leaned toward Epicureanism, he seemed to have softened toward Stoicism in later life. In 1825, only one year before Jefferson's death, a father asked him to give his young son some advice for his life. Jefferson wrote 10 rules that sound decidedly Stoic, down for the son:

"Never put off till tomorrow what you can do today.
Never trouble another for what you can do yourself.
Never spend your money before you have it.
Never buy what you do not want, because it is cheap; it will be dear to you.
Pride costs us more than hunger, thirst, and cold.
We never repent of having eaten too little.
Nothing is troublesome that we do willingly.
How much pain has cost us the evils which have never happened!
Take things always by their smooth handle.

When angry, count ten, before you speak; if very angry, a hundred."

Theodore Roosevelt

The youngest president in America's history had to step into the presidential office when he was not yet 43 years old, after the assassination of President William McKinley in 1901. He overcame ill-health and deeply sorrowful events in his life to become a formidable president.

Roosevelt (1858–1919) was known for exploring trips into wild territories, such as a tributary of the Amazon river called The River of Doubt. On all his journeys he carried Stoic books, such as *The Discourses of Epictetus with the Encheiridion*, with him and made his own notes on the content.

Franklin D. Roosevelt

The 'other' Roosevelt (1882–1945) president was an icon in history, despite contracting polio when he was 39 years old. The disease limited his movements to such an extent that he was always dependent on others for certain things and he eventually ended up in a wheelchair.

He led America through WWII with confidence and calm conviction. One of his widely known quotes is, "Men are not prisoners of their fate, but prisoners of their own minds." This is the way he dealt with his disability, and he performed his duties with the wisdom and patience worthy of any Stoic.

Navy Vice Admiral James B. Stockdale

Vice Admiral Stockdale (1923–2005) became a military pilot in 1950. During the Vietnam War, after having flown more than 200 combat missions already, his plane was shot down. He ejected over a small village in North Vietnam and was captured by enemy soldiers.

He was taken to the infamous prisoner of war camp in Hanoi known as the "Hanoi Hilton," where brutal treatment was dished out regularly. He was kept prisoner for almost eight years and frequently tortured.

Despite having been kept in isolation for four of those eight years, and spending two years in leg irons, Stockdale's resolve to stand up to his captors never wavered. He also inspired the other prisoners.

In later interviews, Stockdale credited Stoicism with giving him the mental, physical, and emotional toughness to survive.

Arnold Schwarzenegger

In a virtual commencement speech Arnold Schwarzenegger (b. 1947) delivered to every one of the class of 2020 who couldn't attend their graduation ceremonies in person because of the coronavirus pandemic, he told them, "It's not about what you are in life, but who."

He also tweeted before the speech, "Life is never perfect but if you have a vision, you will find a way."

The former California governor, also a hugely successful actor and former Mr. Universe, overcame many obstacles since arriving in America from his native Austria at a young age. Penniless, he became a bricklayer to survive. He persevered with bodybuilding and won the amateur Mr. Universe title in 1967, four more professional Mr. Universe titles, and then six Mr. Olympia titles in a row, from 1970 to 1975.

He quoted Marcus Aurelius to the graduating students to remind them character is all that matters. That is the part of life you have control over, not money nor fame nor success.

Other Well-Known Stoics

Well-known authors J. K. Rowling (b. 1965), John Steinbeck (1902–1968), and Ralph Waldo Emerson (1803–1882) all expressed appreciation for the principles of Stoicism.

Rowling said in a tweet that Aurelius had never let her down. Steinbeck mentioned Aurelius' *Meditations* as one of the two books that influenced his life the most. Emerson incorporated several Stoic ideas in his writings.

Chapter 6: On Stoicism, Law of Attraction, and Psychology

Self-help movements, blogs, and groups have never before in history been more popular than now. Spiritualists are fond of speaking about the current time as "the dawn of humankind's enlightenment."

Books like *The Secret* and the law of attraction-movement have gained an immense following in the past two decades, and it shows no sign of stopping.

One of the possible reasons for this might be our fast-changing world with all its political and technological upheavals, with which we have had to learn to cope. Coping with fears and insecurities, surviving emotionally unscathed through your parents' divorce, understanding violence and death, handling the pressure of constant communication in the digital age—these things are not part of a normal school curriculum.

Modern psychology uses many concepts borrowed from self-help movements to connect with modern society in a language that is universally understood.

Could there be a link to Stoicism somewhere?

Law of Attraction

The phrase by which this belief system has become known has its roots in a 19th-century occult book by Helena Petrovna Blavatsky called *The Secret Doctrine*. Blavatsky drew on ancient concepts from Eastern philosophies and Christianity to put forward a theory about how the power of thoughts shapes reality.

The central theme is manifesting desires in concrete form, and the idea really took off in the twentieth century. Well-known books, such as the 1910 publication *The Science of Getting Rich* by Wallace Delois Wattles, and *Think And Grow Rich* by Napoleon Hill (1937), were written during this period.

Rhonda Byrne's *The Secret*, published in 2006, became the best-known source on how to use the law of attraction to everyone's advantage, and not only for a handful of so-called gifted people.

Positive Thoughts and Premeditatio Malorum

One of the cornerstone concepts in the law of attraction (LOA) is to hold positive thoughts only and to focus on positive outcomes. The reasoning behind this is that energy goes where focus goes. Since everything is energy, which makes energy the manifesting power according to LOA, lingering negative thoughts and feelings cancel out the positive thoughts and prohibit the manifestation of good things.

In LOA, worry is a big source of negative energy. The feelings generated by worrying are negative, which lowers the person's energy vibration and invites the very things the worrying is about, to manifest.

While *premeditatio malorum*, or premeditation of evils, is not about manifesting anything, it does concern getting into a state of mind where positive actions can be taken.

Premeditatio malorum is visualizing the worst things you can imagine happening in a specific context. The bad things that are visualized are taken to their logical conclusion, which is to live through them in your mind, surviving them, and solving the problems. That frees the mind from the chains of stress and worry because the expected worst is over and done.

It leaves the Stoic's mind clear and uncluttered by negative emotions so that a positive and virtuous life can again be pursued with conviction.

Fulfilling a Purpose in Life

Stoics have a very definite view of the purpose of living. Pursuing virtue and doing good to others with a calm and cheery disposition, while never shirking from duties, stands out.

Followers of the philosophy are encouraged to use their talents and skills to the benefit of themselves and others, and enjoy their success in doing so.

LOA says we are to enjoy our lives while contributing value to the lives of others. Living with purpose brings positive vibrations, which invite even more success and positive vibrations.

Living this way implies taking action, exactly like Stoicism says. Both these belief systems anchor the actions in *being* first, then taking inspired action. Being implies feelings, which should be controlled to stay positive, according to both systems.

Stoics believe emotions are not merely felt. They also have a rational, judgmental basis, according to Epictetus. We make assumptions or arrive at judgments, which cause us to feel a certain emotion.

LOA teaches its followers that feelings and emotions arise from believing that you already have what you want to manifest before you physically see it—an assumption that the desired object or situation will appear.

The Oneness of All

In both LOA and Stoicism, the universe and all its inhabitants are one. The awareness of this should direct, among other things, our actions toward our fellow man and nature.

Recall that the Stoics thought of the Cosmos as a single, living being. That is why their social duty was extremely important to Stoics throughout the ages. An action in one part of the Cosmos will influence the whole universe.

LOA teaches the same principle of oneness, but their motivation for the concept is their belief that everything is pure energy and nothing else. If we are made from the same substance, we should be one. Therefore, an action toward one part of the Cosmos can change everything in the rest of the universe.

Mindfulness and Gratitude

These concepts play central roles in both LOA and Stoicism. While most people might be more inclined to accept Eastern philosophies as the origin for LOA concepts such as mindfulness, Stoicism has a long Western tradition of mindfulness.

The only difference lies in their perception of what mindfulness is. As discussed before, Stoic mindfulness is verbal—a cognitive awareness. In LOA, the emphasis is on the affective experience of the present moment.

Cognitive Behavioral Therapy

Cognitive behavioral therapy (CBT) is a form of psychotherapy that helps people to look at their own behavior in a logical, reasonable way, and then identify problems and apply solutions.

It is immediately clear that there is common ground with Stoicism. In both systems, control is exerted over the character through the use of reason.

One of the big differences, however, is the fact that CBT is not concerned about moral considerations and a flourishing life like Stoicism is.

Transformation

Both CBT and Stoicism believe transformation through a cognitive modification to behavior is essential for human beings to realize their optimum potential. Although they follow somewhat different routes to get there because of their moral grounding, the result is the same.

To the Stoics, transformation is necessary on universal moral grounds. In CBT, the reason for transformation depends on each client's situation. The client and therapist decide every case on its own merits, while Stoic transformation happens according to a general view of right and wrong that is valid for all mankind.

Chapter 7: Reflections and Meditations

The ancient Stoics did not meditate in the Zen sense of the word, but they had cognitive phrases and concepts they reflected on in a similar state to meditation.

These concepts are rooted in Stoic tradition and common sense. Contemplating them often involved journaling.

In this chapter, there will be some of the classical Stoic reflections that have been around for centuries, as well as one or two more modern, guided meditations.

Reflections

The following were also called exercises, rather than meditations.

Reflecting on the Start of the Day

Experience gratitude for the privilege of having woken up to a new day. Let the grateful feeling flood your being and fully feel it.

Understand and accept that you were given a new opportunity to embrace virtue. Contemplate each virtue and visualize situations in which you can embody each virtue in your daily actions.

Visualize possibilities for doing good to others in line with the primary virtues.

Remind yourself that the only things within your control are your emotions and responses.

***Get Some Perspective*Š

Imagine yourself high above the world, looking down at everyone and everything. You can start as high as you want and gradually come closer to earth.

Observe everything going on without passing judgment. Become aware of the scale of the world and all the people. Reflect on the diversity of actions and emotions taking place all at the same time, from loving and welcoming a first baby, to wars and death, to traffic jams, and artists creating masterpieces.

Remind yourself that you are only a minuscule part of this universe. Everything is relative and the things you hold as matters of life and death today might be forgotten tomorrow.

Try to imagine this exercise in another era. Open up to the realization that a few years back, you did not exist, and in another few years, you will cease to exist. Everything is relative.

Who Is the Ideal Human Being?

All of us have an idea of what the ideal human being should be like. While there are common traits, there are also characteristics that each person finds desirable according to his or her own personality and preferences.

In this reflection, imagine you are looking at your ideal person. Leave physical appearance aside for the moment and focus on the psychological traits this person possesses.

You have the chance of a lifetime to talk to this ideal person. Ask all the questions running through your mind about how to be true to Stoic principles and living a principled life.

Set imaginary scenes and ask your ideal being how they would respond in the situation.

You can also make a list of role models in your life and reflect deeply on the qualities in each that you admire. Ask yourself why you admire particular traits.

Inspire Yourself to Promote the Welfare of Others

The popular interpretation of philanthropy is that only rich people can do it. Money goes far, that is true, but it is not a prerequisite to help fellow human beings.

For this reflection, imagine circles around you. You are in the center and your loved ones are in the circle closest to you. Imagine people in the other circles, ranging from those you care about but who are not family, to your community, to people you only know about. Let the circles increase until you have included every single person on earth in the last circle.

Then visualize pulling a blanket of goodwill over all the circles, enclosing yourself in their midst.

Find Your Inner Peace

Instead of spending thousands of dollars on trips to remote mountains and austere temples, simply journey into yourself. Freedom and peace are within you, and no pilgrimage or any punishing, lonely trip to a distant country will deliver them to you if you are not willing to travel to your own heart.

Sit quietly for ten minutes or so and tune out the world and its sounds. Observe your thoughts as they wander through your mind, without judging or questioning.

Untie the tension knots in your muscles and bask in the peace that is within the stillness of your being.

Peel the Onion

Situations have many layers, just like an onion. What it looks like on the outside, is not necessarily what the core is like.

Reflect on any troubling or puzzling situation in your life right now. Start peeling off layers to get to the heart of the matter. Listen to what your heart is saying. Take note of the outer layers, to understand what needs to be discarded.

Ask yourself if the situation will be adding value to your life, or someone else's. If not, it is not worth your time.

Prepare for the Worst

If you are worried about a possible outcome of any situation, reflect on the worst thing that could happen. Allow yourself to feel it and contemplate how to handle the problems. This technique is called *premeditatio malorum*, or premeditation of evils.

See yourself dissolving the crisis, and feel the personal power emanating from such control.

Often the bad things we imagine don't happen. Let that make your gratitude list even longer.

Remember Death

Reflect on the fleeting moment that is a human being's life on earth. Remind yourself that it certainly will end.

Think about it dispassionately, as a natural part of creation and life.

In the morning, realize that it could be your last day. At night, remind yourself that you might not see the sun again.

Accept the present moment—and the things and people in them—that make you happy, as gifts to be grateful for while they last.

The Flip Side

End your day with a reflection, just as you started it. Take stock of your day. Measure your thoughts and actions against what you set out to achieve that morning.

Don't lose heart if you fell short of your principles. Mentally run through the situation and write a different story this time in your mind.

If you want to start planning the next day, maybe in preparation for the early morning reflection, feel free to do so.

Mindful Meditations

The early Stoics made no mention of mindful meditations because they did not use them. They preferred the reasoning, cognitive activity of reflections. They used the concept of being mindful but in a different context.

Reflections are a verbal and conceptual way of focusing, while meditation in the traditional sense of the word is non-verbal. It can be used to shape our automatic reactions, those responses we do not reason out first.

Meditation can be either a reminder to live true to one's values and the primary virtues, or a powerful nudge in the right direction if the right values have not been cemented yet.

Mindful meditation can also be used to break unhealthy emotional responsive chains. We all have triggers for desires and aversions. To become free of them will require letting go of the triggers and the emotional value we attached to them.

The absence of mindful meditation from ancient Stoic practices does not mean we cannot make use of the new knowledge we have available now for brain training and focusing.

Mindfulness can be described as non-judgmental awareness. It is opening up to perceive everything going on around us without attaching a value to the thought or sensation, or allowing the thought or sensation to color our view of the world.

Mindfulness meditation allows us to soar above our thoughts and emotions to see ourselves as the creations we are—much bigger than our feelings and cognitive processes.

A Typical Mindfulness Meditation

While the method of meditation can vary, there are basic elements such as setting the scene for calmness and relaxation. Some people prefer soft music in the background, while others want complete silence. It is your choice.

You should set aside at least half an hour without distractions and obligations. Choose a spot and position that is most comfortable to you.

If you love the outdoors and it is a nice day, you might want to go outside. On a cold day, a comfortable chair and soft rug in front of the fire might be more suited. Begin:

- Take a few deep breaths and close your eyes

- Breathe in deeply again, and while exhaling, feel all the tension draining from your body with the breath

- If you are a visually-oriented person, you can imagine seeing a white cloud exiting your mouth, containing every bit of tension and stress

- Take a moment just to enjoy the warm, soft feeling of being relaxed

- Bask in the comforting knowledge that you are in control of your emotions and it is, therefore, safe to let go of all your worries and stress

- Reflect for a moment on why you are meditating. What do you want to achieve? A deeper understanding of a specific concept, maybe? Maybe you want to anchor an insight into a difficult situation that you recently had?

- Say to yourself that you will easily return to meditating, should any distractions occur

From this point, you can choose the pattern your meditation will follow. The simplest form of this activity is to focus on your breathing for ten minutes. Experience every inhalation and exhalation fully, and savor the sensation of opening up mentally and physically due to the extra oxygen received by breathing deeply and evenly. If your mind wanders to the stresses of your life while meditating, allow them to flow through you, and send them away. If needed, visualize.

The calm, perceptive state can be useful for planning your day when the meditation is done in the morning.

There are mobile applications and computer programs available to aid meditation. If that will make it easier for you, use them, but don't lose focus on why you want to meditate—to deepen your understanding and mental assimilation of Stoic principles. Allow meditation to lead you to a clearer, more aware, and more purposeful experience of life and the world.

Self-Guided Prompts

On Control

Do I really understand what is under my control in a specific situation, and what is beyond that? Do I have a clear grasp of the things I can change and should spend effort on, and those I should leave alone and continue on my way?

On Equilibrium

How well do I succeed in keeping my emotional equilibrium? Do I keep calm amidst difficult circumstances, or do I allow them to distract me from my purpose? What are my emotional triggers, and how can I think differently about them to avoid them in the future?

On Self-knowledge

Do I really know myself? Am I honest enough with myself to see both my good and bad aspects? Can I list my strengths without unnecessary pride, as well as my weaknesses without falling into the victim trap? How can I turn my weaknesses around to become strengths?

On Duty

Am I using my strengths to their full potential, to fulfill my purpose of living virtuously and doing good to others? Do I use every opportunity I get to be of service, without wishing for recognition or reward? Am I someone who can be counted on in my community and country?

On Objectivity

How do I act when I find that one of my moral judgments is flawed? Do I examine my bias and turn away from it, or do I *arrange the truth to fit into my bias? Am I guilty of confirmation bias?*

Bias in any form sends thoughts and actions in directions that are no longer objective. While it is human to have emotions, the question to ask is whether you are alert to the possibility that emotion may cloud your judgment on some matters. Cognitive behavioral therapy talks about confirmation bias. That refers to the human tendency to look for proof that supports a preconceived idea or opinion.

On Action

Do I progress to decisive action after clear reflection, or do I procrastinate or hesitate? Am I trying to be perfect? Am I unsure of my truth? Am I worried about what others would say if I took action? Am I afraid of any negative consequences to following my Stoic principles?

Epictetus admonished that you first have to know who you want to be, and then you have to do. Seneca joked that the one thing fools have in common is that they are always getting ready to live, but they never do it. Aurelius had to keep reminding himself to stop being aimless and to do everything as if it were the last day. You have to ask yourself first why you hesitate to commence action.

Cognitive behavioral therapy refers to this as cognitive distortions. They are disruptive thought patterns that are detrimental to the patient's well-being and quality of life.

View your life and your progress on life's path objectively. Accept that it is a process and not a singular happening. As long as you have done the best you could for this day, you have not shirked your duty if it turned out to be your last day.

Do what needs to be done on the basis of calm reflection and thorough planning. Prioritize your tasks and set yourself goals and sub-goals.

On Practicality

What are some things in my life that I can pragmatically discard? Are there material things that I am wanting but don't actually need? Why do I want them? Are there relationships that no longer align with who I am? Why do I remain in them?

Aurelius said if a cucumber is bitter, it should be thrown out. It is pointless to hoard useless items.

Collecting clutter to show material wealth is contrary to Stoic principles. Epictetus told us to take just enough to cover our physical needs and nothing more.

The principle of pragmatism also extends to relationships and thought patterns. Those that impede us, rather than helping us grow in virtue, no longer have a place in our lives and should be discarded.

Regular house- and emotional-clearing renews the focus on the four primary virtues and how to put them into practice.

On Kindness

Would others describe me as kind? Am I kind to fellow human beings, animals, and nature? Do I take every opportunity to do good?

While being strict with yourself, your compassion, understanding, and patience should be for the creatures sharing the Cosmos with you. Everything is one, created with the divine presence. A life of kindness honors the oneness of the universe.

On Resilience

Do I rely on luck to get what I want in life, or am I prepared to do the work and walk the rocky road to the garden ahead? Do I allow myself to engage in negative thought patterns? Do I allow the opinions of others to sway me? Do I have a firm grasp of my emotions?

Viktor Frankl said, "When we are no longer able to change a situation, we are challenged to change ourselves." Changing yourself is a hard course to follow. It does not happen overnight, nor does it come without sacrifices. The rewards in peace of mind and clarity of thought throughout your life, and in any situation, outweigh the hardships though. Being prepared for anything means you are always perfectly situated to take advantage of opportunities toward virtue.

Do not stray from your chosen path by allowing external situations that you cannot control to shift your focus. Guard your emotions so they can't derail your resilience either. Do not allow the opinion of other less informed persons to sway you.

Depressive thoughts and anxiety often result from imagining a future that has little chance to come to pass. Reign in your inclination to project negative feelings on a future that only exists in your mind. Be strong in your convictions and reap the peaceful, happy rewards.

Chapter 8: A Week with the Stoics

Stoic teachings are more than a set of rules. It is designed as a philosophy that provides a way to live. It contains practical guidance to navigate everyday occurrences.

Developing the right mindset to live by these principles is a lifelong task which the Stoics set themselves. Doing the same in our modern society can bring emotional equilibrium and peace in a world where these qualities are rare.

Starting every morning with one of the classic Stoic reflections will set the tone for your day and guide your thoughts through difficult situations.

The following is an example of how morning meditations can be made practical. Choose your own and elaborate on them, whether your quotes are from classic writings or modern Stoic collections.

A Quote for Monday

Most people dread Monday mornings. Getting out of bed for work, especially on a winter's morning, has never been easy.

Even someone as dedicated to Stoicism as Emperor Marcus Aurelius experienced that, and he wrote about it in his *Meditations*.

"On those mornings you struggle with getting up, keep this thought in mind—I am awakening to the work of a human being. Why then am I annoyed that I am going to do what I'm made for, the very things for which I was put into this world? Or was I made for this, to snuggle under the covers and keep warm?"

We all have a job to do and that is why we were born into this existence, and in this specific period in earth's history. Humankind is experiencing exceptional challenges in politics, interpersonal relations, and health. Each one of us has a duty in this story, a part to play for the greater good of all. Remember, one bee's good deeds benefit the whole hive.

In a world torn apart by difficulties such as racial tensions, human rights abuses, extreme poverty, hunger, and unemployment, a level head with a generous heart is needed more than ever.

Take Aurelius' words to heart and start your week with the clear intention of doing your job.

Get up, dress up, and show up.

A Quote for Tuesday

Living true to Stoic principles enables you to distinguish between the things that really should and do matter and those that don't deserve your attention.

Anything that does not fall within the four cardinal virtues is a waste of time and should be avoided. Sometimes, ruthless culling is necessary to strip one's life bare of meaningless activities.

Seneca wrote in *On the brevity of life*, "How many have laid waste to your life when you weren't aware of what you were losing, how much was wasted in pointless grief, foolish joy, greedy desire, and social amusements—how little of your own was left to you. You will realize you are dying before your time!"

To say no to anyone is the hardest thing to do for some people. It is, however, necessary sometimes to free the mind and the diary from the clutter that prevents the truth from shining.

Before you accept the next obligation or invitation, measure it against the four primary virtues. Will doing the activity expected of you promote a virtuous life and add to the welfare of all around you?

If not, you know what to do.

A Quote for Wednesday

Not everyone you encounter today will be friendly, helpful, or kind. Your day might bring experiences of hurt or injustice. Be prepared for that, and live your principles regardless.

Aurelius wrote in *Meditations*, "When you first rise in the morning tell yourself: I will encounter busybodies, ingrates, egomaniacs, liars, jealous people, and cranks. They are all stricken with these afflictions because they don't know the difference between good and evil. Because I have understood the beauty of good and the ugliness of evil, I know that these wrong-doers are still akin to me...and that none can do me harm, or implicate me in ugliness—nor can I be angry at my relatives or hate them. For we are made for cooperation."

Stoicism does not expect you to start your day on a negative note. Sometimes, despite our best intentions and actions, things, unfortunately, go awry, and nothing works out as it was supposed to. Aurelius is telling us to be prepared for when the wheels come off, and not be caught off-guard.

Take note of the second part of Aurelius' quote. It is the Stoic way to accept that people differ in opinions and outlooks. Unity can exist in diversity too. While being prepared for being treated unkindly, your attitude toward these people should remain accepting and understanding.

Do not let these happenings cloud your day or shake your resolve to live a virtuous life.

A Quote for Thursday

Everywhere, in almost every house and office, you can hear people complaining about having too little time to accomplish what they have to in a day. Many older folks regret having rushed from task to task, without stopping long enough to enjoy the people and activities that were really important to them.

Seneca taught us, "It is not that we have a short time to live, but that we waste a lot of it. Life is long enough, and a sufficiently generous amount has been given to us for the highest achievements if it were all well invested…Life is long if you know how to use it."

Time on earth is a finite resource, and yet it gets squandered easily. Use your journal to pay attention to all the instances in a day where you used your time on something that had no real value, according to Stoic principles.

Optimize your time well by planning in advance and sticking to those plans. Here again, journaling is an excellent way to plan ahead for your day, and take stock of how well you kept to it at the end of the day.

Fight procrastination by incorporating short-term rewards in your plans. Manage distractions and distinguish between mindless busyness and productive action.

Keep *memento mori* in mind: Spare a thought for death. Today could be your last, use it well.

A Quote for Friday

Is perfectionism one of the demons eating away at happiness in your life?

Consider the following quote from Epictetus: "Don't seek that all that comes about should come about as you wish, but wish that everything that comes about should come about just as it does, and then you'll have a calm and happy life."

Stoics are often accused of being fatalistic. The term carries within it a negative, morbid quality that was never intended by the ancient Stoic philosophers.

Stoicism is deterministic, which means they believe everything is unfolding as it should. It was predetermined by the Divine Fire and that is good and right.

Having a deterministic belief is not paralyzing, though. It all depends on whether you see doing good as a worthy goal to pursue.

Remember Monday's discussion and confirm to yourself that the only measure you have to live up to, is whether you are living a virtuous life. Perfectionism is not attainable, only progress is.

Holding yourself to unrealistic standards that the Cosmos never intended only leads to unhappiness. The preoccupation prevents you from focusing on doing what you are supposed to be doing.

Furthermore, your perception of what is perfect is not the same as your neighbor's perception of it. Even if you reach what you think of as perfection, there will always be someone who sees room for improvement.

Use your journaling practice to plan as thoroughly as you can, and hold yourself accountable at the end of the day for progress.

Be happy in your endeavors to do what is right, and you will live happily and sleep soundly.

A Quote for Saturday

Listen to yourself speak; pay attention to the words you often use. Do you regularly catch yourself saying you *have* to do something?

Today Epictetus tells you, "Disease is an impediment to the body, but not to choice, unless choice wills it to be so. Lameness is an impediment to the leg, but not to choice. And tell yourself the same with regard to everything that happens to you; for you'll find that it acts as an impediment to something else, but not to yourself."

Epictetus was a slave to a brutal master. He was treated cruelly, even by ancient standards. One day his master broke his leg and Epictetus walked with a limp for the rest of his life.

He did not let that make him bitter or deter him from his chosen philosophical path. He remained calmly convinced of his truth and went on to become one of the greatest Stoic teachers that ever lived.

You always have a choice, in everything. There are very few things in life that really have to be done without leaving a choice. Talking and thinking like someone who is imprisoned by circumstances, changes you from a free person to a victim.

Instead, change your conversations to contain "I get to," or, "I want to," while retaining a happy heart and tranquil disposition about the opportunities presented to you each day.

You are in control of your emotions and thoughts. Use your power wisely.

A Quote for Sunday

It's been a long week and it's time to pause and reflect on the past seven days. After the constant rush and noise, many people just try to escape.

Escaping can take several forms, from a physical getaway to losing yourself in activities or substances.

Aurelius' advice on the topic was, "People try to get away from it all—to the country, to the beach, to the mountains. You always wish that you could too. Which is idiotic: You can get away from it anytime you like. By going within. Nowhere you can go is more peaceful—more free of interruptions—than your own soul."

There is no better place to reflect on important aspects of life and philosophy than quietly immersed in your own thoughts.

Chapter 9: Glossary of Terms

The table below contains the Greek words that are used in this book, as a handy reference at a glance. The English equivalents provide the meanings the Stoics gave to the Greek words, rather than merely literal translations.

Greek/Latin word(s)	Phonetic transcription	English equivalent in the Stoic context
ανδρεία	*andreia*	courage
ἀπάθεια	*apatheia*	peace of mind; serenity
δικαιοσύνη	*dikaiosune*	justice
εὐδαιμονία	*eudaimonia*	well-being; a flourishing state
φύσις	*fusis*	psychics; nature
ὁρμή	*hormê*	a positive impulse
λόγος	*logos*	the ordering,

		reasoning principle in the Cosmos
οἰκείωσις	*oikeiosis*	self-awareness
ὄρεξις	*orexis*	desire; longing
πνεῦμα	*pneuma*	spirit; breath of life; created by combining the elements of fire and air
προαίρεσις	*prohairesis*	free will; assent to impressions
προαίρεσις	*prokopê*	progress on the road to wisdom
προσοχή	*prosochê*	attention; Stoic mindfulness
ψυχή	*psychê*	soul; a principle to live by
σοφός	*sophos*	wisdom
σωφροσύνη	*sophrosyne*	moderation

συγκατάθεσις	*sunkatathesis*	assent; agreement
συμπάθεια	*sympatheia*	interdependentness of all things
τέχνη	*technê*	the practical application of Stoic knowledge
premeditatio malorum		premeditation of evils
memento mori		remembering the dead

Conclusion

In some respects, Stoicism was, for its time, far ahead. Maybe that is why its principles endure timelessly, even today.

It advocated a world society and a cosmic consciousness centuries ago. It viewed all humans as equal and entitled to fair treatment.

It cautioned against the consumer mentality that has taken over modern society and ethics, and emphasized the importance of moral qualities over material wealth and status.

Stoics accepted that life happens, and we have to learn to be at peace with it. It taught followers to change what can be changed, and leave the rest be without getting upset over it.

The philosophy stressed the importance of nature and the interconnectedness of all things. This idea of the butterfly effect was popular in ancient Greece and Rome long before modern societies conceived of the idea.

I hope you have enjoyed learning about Stoicism and the power of its philosophies. Go forth and use the wisdom offered in this belief system to your advantage, but also to the advantage and improvement of humankind and the planet.

www.ingramcontent.com/pod-product-compliance
Lightning Source LLC
LaVergne TN
LVHW011737060526
838200LV00051B/3208